What Happens In Vegas...
A Kid's Guide To Las Vegas, Nevada

Photography By John D. Weigand
Poetry By Penelope Dyan

Bellissima Publishing, LLC
Jamul, California
www.bellissimapublishing.com

copyright © 2010 by Penny D. Weigand and John D. Weigand

All rights reserved. No part of this book may be reproduced or transmitted in any form or by any means, electronic or mechanical, including photocopying, recording, or by any other means, or by any information or storage retrieval system, without permission from the publisher.

ISBN 978-1-935630-06-7

First Edition

For Kids Who Love To Have Fun and Explore
And For Parents Who Love
To Have Fun and Explore With Them!

What Happens In Vegas. . .
Bellissima Publishing, LLC

Introduction

Photographer John D. Weigand and author Penelope Dyan went to Las Vegas and came back with another very special travel book meant for kids that will look great on your coffee table. Suffice it to say, this is a new Las Vegas full of lots of surprises as it captures the essence of so many places all over the world! Los Vegas is still the city of lights, but now it is even more!

Entertaining and compact, inexpensive and fun, Las Vegas makes a great place to have a family vacation.

So take a bit of an explore though this book with photographer John D. Weigand and former teacher, author and attorney, Penelope Dyan. When you *see the candy apples*, imagine yourself taking a delectable bite, and when you see the gondolas, imagine yourself taking a ride through the Grand Canal of Venice, Italy!

Purchase this book as a companion book to "Take A Dam Tour! A Kid's Guide To Hoover Dam, Nevada," (also by Dyan and Weigand), and then see and do it all and more with your kids, beginning with the pages of these books. Or you just travel vicariously though this book, because the mind and your imagination can take you anywhere!

Fire up the imaginations of your children with this informative book and ask yourself what kinds of minds created such a diverse, fun and entertaining place that captures the essence of just about everywhere? Perhaps your child will be inspired to become an architect or an artist. You never know where an explore and a dream will lead you!

What Happens In Vegas...
Bellissima Publishing, LLC

What Happens In Vegas...
A Kid's Guide To Las Vegas, Nevada

Photography By John D. Weigand
Poetry By Penelope Dyan

There is a place quite like no other.
And you can go there and see it
with your father and mother.
Or you can go there with your cousins,
your aunt and uncle too,
and when you finally get there,
you will find so much to do!
It's a little bit of New York. . .

And a bit of Venice, Italy too!

Yes, it's even a bit of Paris!
And this is the truth I'm telling you!

In the Rainforest Cafe, an alligator you'll find,
But it's all pretend, so your Mom won't mind!
Or maybe it's a crocodile.
Do you think you'll see it smile?

An elephant may be standing
right over your table.
But he won't eat your food,
because he's simply not able.
He just stands there beneath a plastic tree,
being as fake as he can be!
But I must say when all is said and done,
Eating with any elephant (even a fake one)
is loads of fun!

Nearby you may find a real lion or two
sitting around with nothing to do.
This one was born in captivity,
never knowing what it was like to be free.

Back in the restaurant you will see this snake!
But I must tell you that it, too, is just a fake!

And you can find deserts, buffets
and what's more,
there's even more fun for you
than this in store!

The Excaliber Castle you can see,
You can stay in a room there, or look for free!
They have games inside and all sorts of stuff.
And you can play there 'til you've had enough!

You can go with your folks on a gondola ride,
You can sit across from them or side by side!

You can see a box with a pirate old,
And by him you can have your fortune told.
You just have to know where to look!
And there's lots more stuff not in this book!

You can watch an opera, a funny puppet show,
and there are so many places you can go.
See the marionette climb the stairs,
with the stilted man who has no cares.
Later watch everyone sing and dance,
You have to see this show if you get a chance!

If you want to buy a Venetian mask,
I'm afraid your parents you'll have to ask.

And of course there are lots and lots
of very bright lights,
For you to see on those Las Vegas nights!

And here is something fun to see,
the Las Vegas Lady Liberty!

But please beware of the skull in the cliff,
Because if it moves you must be swift.
Perhaps it hides a hidden treasure,
And protecting it is its one true pleasure.

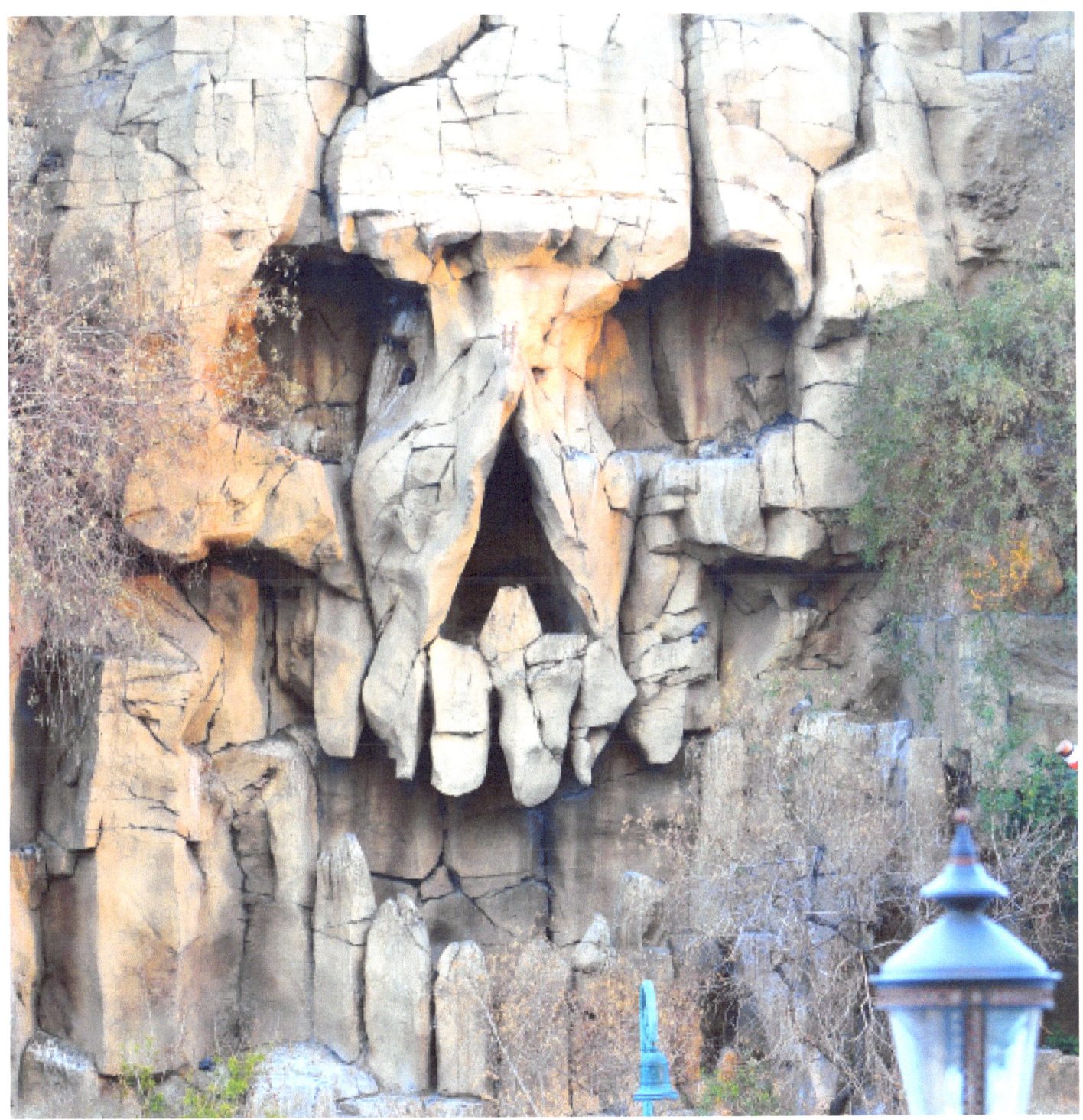

And there is a pirate ship to see all alight,
Shining there for you in the Las Vegas night!

And you can hear the song of the volcano dance.
You must see it erupt if you get a chance!
It is hot and loud and all fiery red,
Reminding you it's time for bed.

And here it is, the best of all,
Go to the Venetian and see the umbrellas fall.
Or are they merely suspended in the air?
They are so beautiful, you just won't care.
They will remind you of your place of dreams,
where nothing is quite just as it seems.
And when to Las Vegas you bid adieu,
Perhaps in a dream they will come to you,
And onto an umbrella handle you'll hold tight,
As you dream and float right through the night.

The End!

Adieu,! Adieu,!
This book is Through!

www.ingramcontent.com/pod-product-compliance
Ingram Content Group UK Ltd
Pitfield, Milton Keynes, MK11 3LW, UK
UKHW060137240426
12048UKWH00002B/77